Is This My Exodus

Lagrange Georgia

Is This My Exodus

written by
Renesheana Blount

Is This My Exodus

Copyright © 2021 by Renesheana Blount

All rights reserved.

No part of this publication may be used or reproduced, stored in a retrieval system, transmitted in any form or by any means-electronic, mechanical, photocopy, recording, or any other except for brief quotations in printed reviews, without the prior written permission of the publisher.

iSeebookz Publishing LLC
Suite 300 Commerce Ave Ste 137B
LaGrange GA. 30241

Editor Y. D. Rowland
Book cover Renesheana Blount

ISBN: 978-1-7347762-5-6

Printed in the United States of America

First edition

10 9 8 7 6 5 4 3 2 1

Minimal editing to maintain authentic integrity.

Acknowledgments

The completion of this undertaking could not have been possible without the participation and assistance of so many people whose names may not be enumerated. Their contributions are sincerely appreciated and gratefully acknowledged. However, I would like to express my deepest appreciation and indebtedness, particularly to the following:

iSeebookz Publishing(my publishing team), Pamela Huguley(My mom), and my beau for their endless support, kind, and understanding spirit during this process.

Above all, the Great Almighty, the author of knowledge and wisdom, for his countless love!

Dedications

*I dedicate this book to God and my mom.
It is because of God's grace and my mom's guidance
that I can glorify Him in this book!*

Depressed, Sad, & Broken,
All these deeds I'm planting
Where's my token?

Crying out for help
Lord, when will it be my time?
I'm so close to giving up,
But I see the finish line.

What's the meaning of family
If a stranger treats you better?
I thought family suppose to be there,
No matter the weather.

Friends ain't the same.
So much betrayal and hate,
I know my exodus is near,
I'm all for the wait.

Failed relationships
Due to lack of trust,
In this world full of love
Why fall for lust?

Is this my exodus, my way out?
Somebody, please point me in the right direction
I promise I'm not here for the clout.
Sickness hit my body
No one to love me at my lowest,
My mom never left my side,
She was the closest.

Diagnosed with Impetigo
Skin all in a mess,
There's nothing in this world
That could make me feel any less.

Is this my exodus, my departure?
It seems to me I'm being tortured.

I couldn't take it anymore,
I was at my lowest.
No one cared for real,
My heart became the coldest.

Despite what I went through
Keeping everyone else lifted,
I turned my head, asking for help
And it's like the whole world shifted.

Is this my exodus?
I'm always there for others.
When will it be the time for my hidden talents to be uncovered?

Never been close to father.
No hate in my heart,
It's a shame we don't even know what tore us apart.

Indecisive about my career,
Can't see the 10-year vision,
"Do this, Rene, do that, Rene."
Surrounded by all this tension.

Self-conscious about my weight gain
I knew one day I would start to pick up.
I just didn't expect all the criticism,
Please don't get me started on Trump.

Is this my exodus; my reflow, my flight
I'm almost at the end.
I see the light...

People praying on my downfall
They think they know me so well,
But with the Lord on my side
I will never fail.

Anxiety trying to get the best of me
Not knowing what tomorrow brings.
I know God will fight this battle for me.
He is my King!

Denied my power because of the color of my skin,
For God turned my enemies into my footstools,
I always Win!

Is this my exodus, my discharge, my emigration?
To some, my all isn't still quite good enough,
I need a vacation.

Sure people love the recognition, the publicity the spotlight.
Pay attention to that kind,
because when it's your time to be recognized,
They are nowhere to be found.

Giving up isn't an option.
Philippians 4:13
Whenever I am down and out
God has a shoulder where I can always lean.

Is this my exodus?
I need to find my exit.
Crying out from time to time,
Makes me feel so desperate.

In and out of church
Trying to deal with the hypocrites,
Church should be one big family,
Not all these separate clicks.

I salute my mom
She's the strongest lady I know.
Through all the trials & tribulations
God still loved her so.

Siblings ain't close No'more.
I'm thankful for the bond I share with mine.
We can have a million things going on,
But we still find the time.

Is this my exodus?
I'm starting to see things a little clear.
Back then, it use to be rough for me
But I'm claiming this will be my year.

Removed, but I forgave the people that hurt me,
No more shackles, no more chains

i know my worth, but i choose to settle.
Accepting less than what i deserve is like dancing with the devil.

Tired of being lied to, tired of the games,
It's hard to find someone that wants the same.

i laugh to keep from crying.
i'm busy, so my mind won't wonder,
Hanging out, chilling with family
Somehow my mind begins to ponder.

Could that be depression?
Could that be anxiety?
Could that be bi-polarness?
Maybe I should reach out to society.

Is this my exodus?
I thought I was finding my exit.
Lord please find my soul, and try your best to cleanse it.

Feeling resentful,
But I know Karma is real.
You couldn't pay me to be low down
Jail is not where I want to have my meals.

One second I'm up,
The next I'm down,
Dealing with all these issues
Trying to find the smile through my frown.

Why can't I trust?
For a relationship, it's a must.
The past got me so broken,
For this matter right here, I'll remain unspoken.

Homeboys first,
Us good women last.
I'm tired of this roller coaster of love,
It's like I'm reliving my past.

Embarrassed to show me off,
Do i not meet your standards?
Why choose to be with me,
If my name is to be slandered.

Sometimes i feel like I'm too loyal.
I don't get the same in return.
All these lessons I'm being taught.
When am i going to learn?

I'm up; then I'm down.
You would think it was some kind of disorder.
I'm tired of these repetitive problems.
During these times, i need a supporter.

Is this my exodus?
I'm still dealing with pain and anger,
At this point, i just need my soul anchored.

What a world we live in
All these senseless killings.
Parents scared to send their kids to school.
Cruel acts during this time may never be forgiven.

Lord knows I'm trying to make something out of myself.
Hard to stay on track when things start to go left.

Is this my exodus, my going out?
You will make a way, Lord
I have no doubt.

Still not finished with college,
RN is what I'm claiming.
I'm trying my best to get that title.
But first, I must stop complaining.

Loving my job, co-workers, and patients.
But it's something about management,
Who's always searching for replacements.

Writer's block was just what I needed.
It gave me more time to gather my thoughts.
Losing my ability to produce new work,
Just gave me more material to write about

Is this my exodus, my discharge, my drain?
Things are starting to get more clearer.
So much knowledge I've gained.

Silent cries from relatives.
Good thing I can lend a helping hand,
I'll always be one phone call away
For family, I'll drop everything that's planned.

Comparing my life to social media
I had to fast from that.
The mind is a terrible thing to waste,
That is something that i must not lack.
Most times, I felt attacked.

Trying to keep ME busy,
So I won't think toxic.
But when I say what's on THE mind,
I'm psychotic.

Waking up some days feeling so useless,
Wishing i could go back to sleep.
Receiving a phone call from my mom,
Makes life more continuous.

Is this my exodus; my way out of depression?
Some days are better than others,
I have so many confessions.

We live to embrace death,
Be completely present in it.
Life is a timespan short,
Makeup, recommit and forgive it.

Keep people in your corner,
Wanting the same as you.
Some people will be permanent.
Some you thought you knew...

"I have decided to stick with love."
"Hate is is too great a burden to bear."
That's my favorite quote from Dr. Martin Luther King Jr.
It seemed like he was the only one in the world that gave a care.

Is this my exodus?
Why must history repeat itself,
We will never move forward until we find love within ourselves.

Claiming you love someone
But being dirty behind their back.
You get mad when you get caught,
Now you feel so attacked.

You can't trust anyone,
Not even those who trust you.
People will take the majority of your earnings,
And leave you with only a few.

Putting my life on hold
While waiting for others,
Got used to my last dime
I am still trying to recover.

Depression never leaves
You just find ways to cope.
Trying to have a normal life,
Just brings false hopes.

Is this my exodus?
It's hard to exit this narrow path.
Life is what you make it though
I will push through until my last breath.

Be happy don't give up, reinvent yourself.
Never feel like you are all alone,
There is always someone to help.

I admire my baby sister,
Even though I'm the oldest,
She's taught me to stay strong,
No matter how much people throw dust.

Personages I used to call my sister and brother,
Walk past me like I'm a ghost.
Did I outgrow them, or did they outgrow me,
Who knows?

Reaching out to me when it's convenient for you.
Did you forget I need help too?

Asking for money
When you know I'm on my last ten.
This giving thing should be mutual,
If you expect me to lend.

Is this my exodus
To get used?
Thinking I'm gonna get played again,
You got me confused.

Brighter days are ahead
That is my 20/20 vision.
If life tries to knock me down again,
I'll take it as just an intermission.

Time waits for no one,
So why put a hold on your goals.
Make your dreams your reality,
You'll never know how your life unfolds.

Is this my exodus, my withdrawal?
Life, why won't you stop for me,
Am I too young for menopause?

If you're not dead, God is not done.
Some days you'll look back
On the victories, you've won.

Break down sometimes
Let the tears all out,
Cancel plans, say no,
Have you some "Me" time.

Take the next step, even though it's scary.
There will be trials
No On the contrary,
There will be tribulations.

No matter the risks ahead
Take the next step,
With God
You'll have all the help.

Set back for a comeback,
We have all been there and done that,
Made mistakes-
But also made an impact.

Is this my exodus?
My fleeing...
Too much thought on this could interrupt my well-being.

Ever heard of a twin flame?
More like a twin soul.
It's like when you finally meet your match
Who makes your heart whole.

Needless to say, I've finally found my love,
Jesus being the first
He's the second-best thing
That has ever happened to me.

He saw my heart and healed it.
We have a bright future ahead of us,
This is what I foresee.

Love is a gamble, not a game.
You're supposed to take some risks, not play.
Be honest and truthful with your partner.
That hard work you put in will definitely pay off.

Is this my exodus, my exit?
Everything is beginning to make sense now,
With life being so challenging, I know what not to allow.

Absent from social media has changed me mentally.
All the drama that's circulating the world
What I do, there is absolute confidentiality.

Move unnoticed
Keep your dreams silenced.
Keep grinding
You'll always remain the highest.

Find your exodus in negativity.
Your way out will show you new possibilities.
Learn to be cool and calm about everything,
Don't let the world stop you from it's deterring.

This talk about the coronavirus
Has got everyone distracted.
People claim it's something that's man-made.
Whatever it is, I don't want to contract it.

The high rate of STD's is now among us.
Something we can't run from
We must discuss it.

Sleeping with this and that person is so easy to do
Let's take care of our bodies more.
Take time to listen,
It will always give off clues.

Is this my exodus?
It could be yours as well,
Lord forgive us of our sins,
We don't want our souls in hell.

Make a wish on 11:11
At least i believe in superstition.
Free your mind and
Trust your intuition.

Read your zodiacs
Read your fortunes
Study your life
But avoid the misfortunes.

I am down to 4 people, in my corner.
I take this life of mine serious,
Somebody should have warned you.
I don't mind being alone,
Peace is all I'm searching.
My happiness comes before anything,
I know i am well deserving.

*Is this my exodus
I feel like my breakthrough is coming.*

For God sent his only begotten son
To save me of my shortcomings!

I'm not always right,
Nor do I think I'm better.
I just finally know my worth
Everything is starting to come together.

If you're not dating to marry
Then what are you dating for,
If you can't see a future
Move on and explore.

Bitter baby mommas,
Stop the madness.
Co-parenting is easy,
Don't fault a good father
Because of your sadness.

My exodus is dear
Me finding my way is really near.

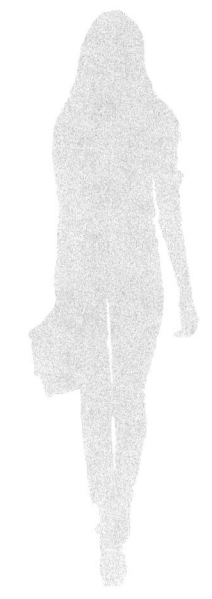

I don't want to give up something I'm so good at
Sticking people is no longer where my heart is at.

Management brag on me all the time,
About how good of a phlebotomist I am.
It's time for me to move on now,
Having this job has really had my mind in a cram.

So many opportunities that I have yet to explore,
Deep down might be some discouragement.
But God will always open up a door.

More rest, clear skin, and positive thoughts
No more being distraught.

Increased finances, earned degrees.
This year is mine
I finally feel at ease.

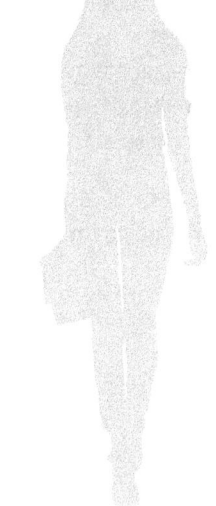

Some stuff you got turned away from
Some stuff you got to turn off.
Some people you got to keep behind you
Because of all the negativity, it brought.

Apply for that job you want
Get that car you keep looking at,
Start your New Years' resolution in June.
Just don't backtrack.

It's never too late to get yourself together.
We're all one big happy family.
Think about the birds of a feather
Life is too short to live it unhappily.

I've come this far by faith.
Leaning on the Lord
Trusting that he'll make a way,
For sure, I have been restored,

Never thought my exodus would have an end.
But here it is so sad to say,
I have been through hell and high waters,
Through it all, I still remain okay!

Author Biography

Renesheana Blount is a Native American from Valley, Alabama. She studied at West Georgia Technical College(Lagrange, Georgia), where she received her certification in phlebotomy, and she also has her certificate in Medical Assistant. She is currently in school, completing her BSN in Nursing.

In 2017 she released her first Prayer Journals. Journaling, writing short stories, and writing personal poetry has always been her passion. Her self-driven attitude gave her the boost she needed to complete her first personal poetry book, "Is This My Exodus." Only time will tell what will take place next, but until then, she will keep putting her creative thoughts to use and continue to write to keep her readers captivated.

www.ingramcontent.com/pod-product-compliance
Lightning Source LLC
Chambersburg PA
CBHW071326080526
44587CB00018B/3353